D1361174

How Do They Grow?

From Puppy to Dog

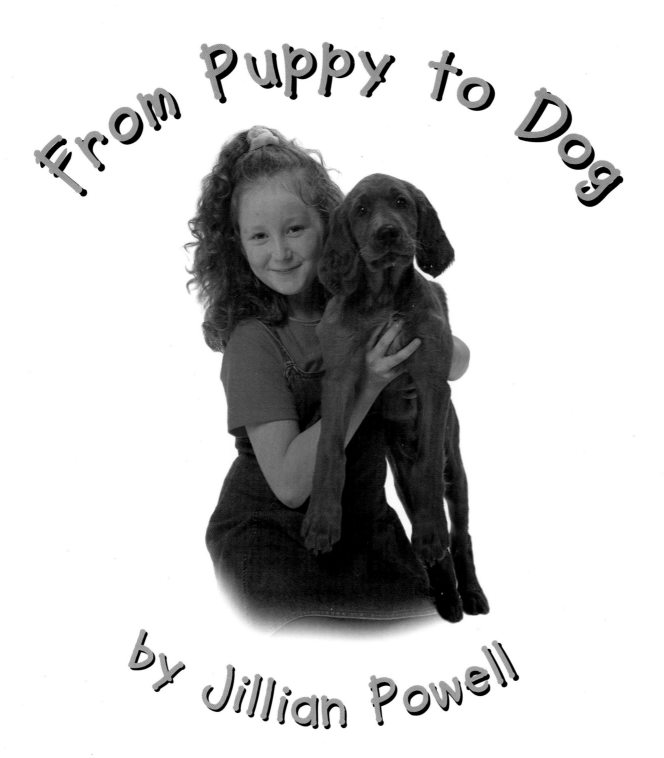

by Jillian Powell

RAINTREE
STECK-VAUGHN
PUBLISHERS

A Harcourt Company

Austin   New York
www.steck-vaughn.com

Published by Raintree Steck-Vaughn Publishers, an imprint of Steck-Vaughn Company

Library of Congress Cataloging-in-Publication Data
Powell, Jillian.
From puppy to dog / by Jillian Powell.
    p. cm.—(How do they grow?)
    Includes bibliographical references and index.
    ISBN 0-7398-4423-7
    1. Puppies—Juvenile literature. 2. Dogs—Development—Juvenile literature. [1. Dogs. 2. Animals—Infancy. 3. Pets.]
    I. Title.

    SF426.5 .P69 2001
    636.7'07—dc21   00-054296

Printed in Italy. Bound in the United States.
1 2 3 4 5 6 7 8 9 0 05 04 03 02 01

Picture acknowledgments
Angela Hampton Family Life Picture Library 10, 11, 12, 16, 17, 19, 21, 24, 25, 28; NHPA 7 (E. A. Janes), 26 (Yves Lanceau); HWPL title page; Oxford Scientific Films 4 (Liz Bomford), 5 (Clive Bromhall), 6 (Michael Leach), 14 (Daniel J. Cox), 23 (Renee Stockdale/Animals Animals), 27 (Zig Leszczynski/Animals Animals), 29 (J. L. Klein & M. L. Hubert/Okapia); RSPCA Photolibrary 8 (Cheryl A. Ertelt), 9 (Cheryl A. Ertelt), 13 (Angela Hampton), 15 (Angela Hampton), 18 (Angela Hampton), 20 (Angela Hampton).

Contents

Words in **bold** in the text can be found in the glossary on page 30.

Puppies Are Born

A puppy is born. It is the first in a **litter** of puppies. The mother licks her puppy. This helps it to start breathing.

The puppy is tiny and wet. It can smell and feel its mother. The puppy cannot yet hear or open its eyes.

The Puppies Start to Grow

These puppies are drinking their mother's milk. This helps them grow strong and fight off **germs**.

These puppies have grown bigger. As they grow,
their legs become stronger, and they can walk.

Becoming Active

This puppy is four weeks old. The puppy learns by using its eyes and ears.
It also has a very good sense of smell.

Puppies love playing together.

They soon get tired and need to sleep.

Growing First Teeth

This puppy is six weeks old. It has its **milk teeth** and can start to eat puppy food. It has four small meals a day.

A puppy loves to bite and chew.

This helps to keep its teeth clean and strong.

Ready for a New Home

This puppy is eight weeks old and ready to leave its mother. The puppy will need lots of love and care from its new owner.

A new owner must care for a puppy like a new mother. The puppy needs clean bowls of food and water every day.

A Visit to the Vet

Puppies must visit the vet before they can meet other dogs. The vet checks that the puppy is healthy.

He is giving this puppy a **vaccination**. This
will keep it safe from catching diseases when
it goes outdoors.

Being Outdoors

The puppy can start to explore its new home. Its nose learns new smells. It knows the smell of its home and of its owner.

The puppy loves running and playing.

It needs to have exercise every day.

This helps it grow strong and healthy.

Playing with Toys

Playing with toys helps the puppy to learn. It likes to show how strong it is by playing **tug-of-war** with its owner.

18

The puppy loves to chase and catch toys. Its owner throws it a ball to fetch but never sticks or stones. These may hurt the puppy.

Puppy Training

The puppy's owner takes it to puppy school. It meets other puppies there and learns to get along with them.

A puppy is taught to sit and stay. The puppy understands when its owner is pleased. It also learns to walk on a leash.

Grooming and Bathing

A puppy needs to be **groomed** to keep its coat clean and healthy. Its owner brushes out old fur every week.

The puppy licks its fur to keep it clean. Sometimes it gets its fur very dirty and needs a bath.

Food and Drink

The growing puppy now eats bigger meals twice a day. A puppy needs plenty of clean water, too.

Sometimes, its owner gives a puppy a special treat, such as a dog biscuit. A treat can be a **reward** when the puppy is learning.

A Puppy Becomes a Dog

These puppies have grown into young dogs.

Their bodies have grown longer and firmer.

Their legs are longer and stronger, too.

26

A young dog can hear the tiniest sounds.
It sniffs the air where it can pick up
different smells.

Having Puppies

This female dog is going to have puppies.
She **mated** with a male dog, and the puppies
began growing inside her.

After nine weeks the puppies are born. The mother will feed, wash, and look after them. Each puppy will grow up to be a strong, healthy dog.

Glossary

Germs (jurmz) Tiny particles around us that can carry diseases.

Groomed (groomd) When an animal's fur has been brushed and combed.

Litter (LIT-ur) All the young animals born to the same mother at the same time.

Mated (MAY-ted) When a male and female have come together to have babies.

Milk teeth The first teeth that a baby animal or person grows.

Reward (ree-WARD) Something that is given when a person or an animal has done well.

Tug-of-war (tug-uv-wor) A game where two sides pull a rope away from each other as hard as they can.

Vaccination (VAC-suh-nay-shun) An injection given with a needle into the skin. A vaccination protects animals and people from diseases.

Further Information

Books

Doudna, Kelly. *Puppies*. Sandcastle, 2000.

Head, Honor. *Puppy*. Raintree Steck-Vaughn, 2000.

Otto, Carolyn. *Our Puppies Are Growing: Stage 1*. Harper Collins, 1998.

Starke, Katherine. *Dogs and Puppies*. EDC Publications, 1999.

Vrbova, Zuza, and Sandra Stotsky. *Puppies*. Chelsea House, 1998.

Websites

www.aspca.org

The official site of the American Society for the Prevention of Cruelty to Animals (ASPCA), with lots of useful information on pet care.

www.lurch.net/pets.htm

A site which gives you advice about how to care for your pet. It also includes pages on the care of your dog plus games, stories and crafts.

Useful addresses

American Society for the Prevention of Cruelty to Animals
424 East 92nd Street, 4th Floor
New York, NY 10128-6804

Index